A Fortunate Storm

THE IMPROBABLE STORY OF STOICISM:
HOW IT CAME ABOUT AND WHAT IT SAYS

Dr. Chuck Chakrapani

The Stoic Gym Publications

Copyright © 2016 by Chuck Chakrapani.

All rights reserved. No part of this publication may be reproduced, distributed or transmitted in any form or by any means, including photocopying, recording, or other electronic or mechanical methods, without the prior written permission of the publisher, except in the case of brief quotations embodied in critical reviews and certain other noncommercial uses permitted by copyright law. For permission requests, please contact: www.ChuckChakrapani.com

The Stoic Gym
A Standard Research Systems Imprint

For bulk ordering and rights permissions requests, please visit http://thestoicgym.com.
First Edition.
ISBNs
Print: 978-0-920219-10-2
ePub: 978-0-920219-11-9
Mobi: 978-0-920219-12-6
PDF: 978-0-920219-13-3

25 24 23 22 21 20 19 18 17 16   1 2 3 4 5 6 7 8 9

Unshakable Freedom

A Companion Volume to A Fortunate Storm

A Fortunate Storm is the story of how Stoicism came about. UNSHAKABLE FREEDOM shows how Stoic teachings can be used to achieve unshakable freedom in your life right now, no matter what problems you are facing in your life.
Available now at your favorite online bookstore

Contents

The Strange Story of Stoicism 1

The Story of a Shipwreck 5

    "It was a dark and stormy night." 5

    Follow that man! 6

    The man Zeno followed around 6

    I am Diogenes, the dog! 7

    Diogenes the dog 8

    Zeno's quest for knowledge 10

    Crates' outrage 11

    The porch philosophers 12

    Softening Cynicism 13

    A fortunate storm 15

The Story of the Seven Scholarchs 17

    Five hundred years of Stoic thought 17

    Zeno to God: Why do you call me? 19

    Cleanthes: The boxer takes over 20

- Chrysippus, the long-distance runner, follows 22
- Zeno of Tarsus 26
- Diogenes of Babylon 27
- Antipater of Tarsus 28
- Panaetius of Rhodes, the last scholarch 29
- Non-Stoic heroes of Stoicism 30
- Cicero, the polymath 32
- Stoicism moves to Rome 33

The Story of a Slave and an Emperor (and Two Others) 37
- Seneca, the exile who tutored an emperor 38
- Rufus, the third founder of Stoicism 41
- Epictetus, philosophy's most famous slave 43
- Aurelius, the Emperor inspired by a slave 44

The Story of the Survival of Stoic Works 49
How I Came to Write This Book 53
- Unshakable Freedom: What They are Saying 57

ABOUT THE AUTHOR 60

INTRODUCTION

The Strange Story of Stoicism

Strange is the story of Stoicism.

Three unconnected events – a shipwreck in Piraeus, a play in Thebes, and the banishment of a rebel in Turkey – connected three unrelated individuals to give birth to a philosophy. It was to endure two thousand years and offer hope and comfort to hundreds of thousands of people along the way.

Stoicism had seven formal leaders or "scholarchs," but much of what we know of Stoicism today comes from four Stoics who lived after the all the scholarchs were gone.

This is the story of those eleven people. Many others contributed to Stoicism, but to make this a readable story and not a compendium of facts, I have confined myself to the seven scholarchs and the four prominent late Stoa figures.

The story of the scholarchs is not validated history but based on anecdotal evidence. This is not a history book, but a loose reconstruction of past events based on second or third-hand evidence and unconfirmed stories. The sources I consulted (some of them secondary) are provided at the end under Notes. When I came across contradictory versions of the same event, I chose the one that sounded more plausible or more interesting. Where details of events are of no special importance, I have used my imagination to tell the story and connect the dots. I would assume, while the details are open to question, the main events are probably true.

The strangeness of Stoics runs through their history as a connecting thread. The early scholarchs included a wealthy businessman, a poverty-stricken professional boxer, and a brilliant long-distance runner. The later proponents included the most powerful man in the world in his time, a powerless slave whose legs were broken by his master, and a royal advisor whose misfortune it was to be the advisor to a mad tyrant.

It is hard to conceive of a group of people so dissimilar and so unique. These were the people who founded and nurtured Stoicism. They worked on solutions to the problems of living and found answers. This philosophy worked for the rich and the poor; for the sickly and the vibrantly healthy; and for the most powerful and least powerful. No wonder the answers they found have illumined the paths of seekers over two thousand years and continue to do so today.

If you are not familiar with Stoic philosophy, here it is in a nutshell as I understand it.

STOIC PHILOSOPHY: ONE MINUTE INTRODUCTION

You can be free, happy, and serene, no matter what else is happening around you, if you understand this basic truth: some things in life are under your control, and others are not.

These things are under your control: What you believe, what you desire or hate, and what you are attracted to or avoid. You have complete control over these, so they are free, not subject to restraint or hindrance. They concern you because they are under your control.

These things are not under your control: Your body, property, reputation, status, and the like. Because they are not under your total control they are weak, slavish, subject to restraint, and in the power of others. They do not concern you because they are outside your control. The window of control we have may appear small but is large enough to lead us to freedom, happiness, and serenity.

Everything that happens around you or to you is part of reality. You need to deal with reality using things that are under your control. When you try to deal with reality using things not under your control, you will be hindered and frustrated.

If you lead your life confining yourself only to things that are under your control, no one can stop you from being free, happy, and serene.

If you want these substantial rewards in life, you should be prepared to put in the effort. This means you may have to give up some things entirely and postpone others for now. If you attempt to get both what is under your control and what is not, you may end up getting neither. Therefore, you clearly need to distinguish the two.

How do you tell the difference? Start by challenging everything that appears disagreeable. "You are only an appearance. Let me fully understand what you are." Then, using the distinction we talked about, examine it to see if it is under your total control. If it is not within your control, it is nothing to you; there's nothing to worry about.

CHAPTER 1

The Story of a Shipwreck

"It was a dark and stormy night."

More than three hundred years before the birth of Christ, a merchant ship loaded with purple dye was making its way from Citium in Cyprus to Athens. As the ship approached Piraeus, it was caught in a storm, and shipwrecked. Not an unusual incident in those days. It would have been long forgotten but for the fact that there was, among the survivors, a young man, twenty-two years of age. His name was Zeno.

Zeno was the son of Mnaseas, a purple dye merchant who frequently traveled to Athens. Whenever he returned, he brought his son books[1] about the famous philosopher, Socrates. The young Zeno was fascinated by the famous philosopher.

Zeno, born the same year as Emperor Alexander, took up his father's trade but after the shipwreck he made his way to Athens. There he met a bookseller who was reading the second book of Xenophon's Memorabilia of Socrates. On reading it, Zeno decided to give up his former profession and study philosophy instead.

Follow that man!

But there was a problem. Socrates had been dead for several years. Who would Zeno study with? He asked the bookseller where one could find a man like Socrates. The bookseller looked up and saw Crates of Thebes passing by the bookstore.

"Follow that man over there!", the bookseller exclaimed.

Zeno followed Crates and studied with him. Zeno sold his business and cargo and remained in Athens for the remaining fifty years of his life.

The man Zeno followed around

Crates, like Zeno, was the son of a wealthy family in Thebes. One day he saw a play of the Tragedy of Telephus.

The story was about King Telephus, son of Heracles, who was wounded by Achilles. The wound would not heal, so Telephus consulted the oracle. The oracle told him the wound could only be healed by the one who inflicted it. Disguising himself as a beggar, Telephus went to Achilles' camp and convinced Achilles to heal him with the same spear that wounded him.

Crates was moved by this play, perhaps because it showed no one is immune to pain and loss, even a king and the son of a demigod.

After seeing the play, Crates gave away his personal wealth to the people of Thebes, left his family, and went to Athens to study philosophy. There he met and studied with Diogenes of Sinope. We will come back to Diogenes later in this chapter.

Crates taught by example and discussions in the streets of Athens. He became known as "the door opener"[2] because he would walk into people's homes uninvited, give them counsel if they faced any problem, resolve the situation, and then leave. Although he was physically unattractive, his generosity of spirit and cheerfulness made him welcome in many homes.

To Crates, anything that was not part of nature was a trap. Such traps included social etiquette, social status, and wealth. When his family tried to persuade him to return to his former life of ease and luxury in Thebes, he is said to have driven them away with a stick.

Crates was a Cynic philosopher. The word cynic now means "a person who believes people are motivated purely by their self-interest rather than acting for honorable or unselfish reasons." But it meant something entirely different in those days.

I am Diogenes, the dog!

Cynicism is a school founded by Antisthenes, a disciple of Socrates. Cynics led an austere life, avoiding ease and pleasure. They lived on the streets of Athens. They had contempt for social conventions and customs. For them "living according to nature" was the only way to live. In their minds, everything else was arbitrarily made up by society. They did not mind a way of life that was looked down upon. They did not care what anyone else thought of them.

In fact, the word Cynic was derived from the Greek words for 'dog' and 'dog-like,' presumably an insult thrown at them for their shameless way of life. Just as you would expect, Cynics accepted the name instead of being insulted by it.

Cynicism offered a way to achieve happiness and freedom from suffering. Although there was no manifesto of the Cynic school, here is a summary of what they believed[3] constituted the good life (eudemonia):

> HOW TO FLOURISH ACCORDING TO CYNICS
>
> Have mental clarity and be free from ignorance, mindlessness, folly, and conceit.
>
> To achieve mental clarity do ascetic exercises.
>
> Live according to nature, as defined by reason.
>
> Avoid arrogance. It is caused by false judgments and results in negative emotions, unnatural desires, and vicious character.
>
> Cultivate self-sufficiency, love of humanity, excellence, candidness, and indifference to life's ups and downs.
>
> Practice shamelessness to reject societal norms.

Diogenes the dog

The most famous practitioner of Cynicism at the time was Diogenes of Sinope, Crates' teacher. Diogenes in turn had been a follower of Antisthenes, the leader of the Cynics. Diogenes was born in Sinope (Sinop in modern day Turkey), an Ionian colony in the Black Sea around 400 BCE (give or take a dozen years). His father was a banker called Hicesias who minted coins for a living.

The young Diogenes took to the debasement of currency which did not sit well with the powers-that-be, and he was banished. His possessions were taken away, and he lost his citizenship.

And so Diogenes moved to Athens accompanied by Manes, a slave. It is not clear why, perhaps the company of Diogenes was too much for the slave, but one day he disappeared without warning.

Diogenes put on a brave face and said: "Well if Manes could live without Diogenes, why not Diogenes without Manes?"

As soon as he settled in Athens, Diogenes resumed his disruptive ways. He started criticizing local customs and conventions. To make his point that the society was corrupt, he used his simple lifestyle as the model. He pulled several stunts to make his statement: he would beg for food and eat anything; he lived in a large ceramic jar in the marketplace; he would go to lectures by Plato and sabotage his talks by challenging his interpretation of Socrates; he would distract the attendees of Plato's talks by bringing food and eating it loudly during the discussions[4]. Plato may have been a great philosopher for others, but to Diogenes, he was just another guy with incorrect ideas.

Diogenes also pulled a lot of philosophical stunts. When followers of Plato defined humans as "featherless bipeds," he plucked the feathers of a chicken and threw them at the academics saying, "Here's your Platonic human!" To further mock the Platonists, he went around carrying a lamp in the daytime looking for a "human being." In spite of all his shenanigans, or because of them, he became a famous philosopher of his day.

Diogenes, like his mentor Antisthenes, rejected material wealth, objects, and social status. Instead, he emphasized a life of simplicity lived according to nature. Personal possessions were unnecessary because they distracted one from living one's life according to nature. The same was true of social status, formal education, and social etiquette. Human beings artificially conceived these concepts. Diogenes believed they prevented people from living honest lives.

Alexander the Great heard about and came to visit Diogenes, the famous philosopher. Diogenes was not particularly impressed. The dialog between them went something like this:

"I am Alexander the Great."

"I am Diogenes the Dog."

"Can I do anything to make your life better?"

"Yes, please move over, don't hide the sun."

Diogenes was mocking Alexander. When Alexander described himself as Alexander "the Great", Diogenes responded by calling himself a dog. When Alexander offered anything Diogenes wanted, he suggested he had everything if only Alexander would go away.

Crates was a student of Diogenes, but Diogenes lived on the street. He owned no building, ran no conventional school. Nor, as someone who made a virtue of poverty, would Diogenes have rented a place. Crates probably learned from his master not in a traditional way but by observing his behavior.

Street life was as tough in those days as it is now. While living in the streets of Athens, Diogenes was captured and sold into slavery. He then settled in Corinth and, when the time came, passed on the mantle to Crates of Thebes. It is this Crates our hero Zeno met and followed around.

Zeno's quest for knowledge

Zeno (334 – 262 BCE) was a good student, although he struggled with some aspects of Cynicism such as shamelessness.

To free Zeno from his embarrassment Crates gave Zeno a pot of lentil soup to carry through the Ceramicus, the potter's quarter of Athens. Crates noticed that Zeno was ashamed of the task and tried to hide the pot under his clothes. Crates broke the pot with a staff making the soup flow down Zeno's legs, causing him even more embarrassment.

Crates responded to this by saying, "Why run away, my little Phoenician? Nothing terrible has happened to you!" Gradually Zeno overcame his inhibitions to become shameless.

But Zeno didn't stop at studying Cynicism. While he learned it well and absorbed its teachings, he also visited competing schools of philosophies, and attended their lectures, such as the Megarian, the Dialectical, and even the Platonist philosophy.

Crates' outrage

Philosophers in those days demanded their protégés' loyalty. When Crates heard Zeno was attending other schools, he was outraged. He went looking for Zeno and found him at the Megarian School with Stilpo. Crates started physically dragging Zeno away from Stilpo.

Zeno argued, "Crates, the sophisticated way to get a hold on philosophers is by ears [logical arguments]; but if you use force on me, my body will be with you and my soul with Stilpo."

The Megarian School was founded by Euclides of Megara, who had been a pupil of Socrates. Euclides' philosophy was a fusion of Eleatic and Socratic schools of thought. The Megarians held that what matters is the moral good and the will of the good person to strive towards it. Stilpo taught freedom, self-control, and self-sufficiency in a way similar to Cynics' thinking.

The Dialectical School emphasized the logic of arguments and made contributions to modal logic and conditional statements. They developed propositional logic, which became the precursor of Stoic logic when Zeno later combined the best of different philosophic systems of his time. He was so impressed with logic as taught by the Dialectical School that he would declare it a virtue later.

The porch philosophers

Zeno had just turned 33 in 301 BCE. He decided he was knowledgeable enough to strike out on his own. He didn't care to establish an exclusive school. He wanted to discuss his philosophy from a space unobstructed by bystanders, in the cynical tradition. He chose the porch on the North side of the Athenian marketplace or agora and started sharing his ideas.

The porch or stoa under which Zeno set up his shop was known as the painted porch (because of a painting by Polygnotus) or stoa poikile. This was not exactly a prime location. Thirty tyrants and 1,400 citizens were executed there. Yet people came to listen to him because his teachings were popular. Anyone who was interested in his ideas was welcome to join the gathering. Zeno came to Athens as a philosophic nobody and ended up establishing a school of philosophy that would endure more than two millennia after him.

Zeno believed happiness should be based on reason and not on fulfilling every desire that arose in the mind. A wise person was not free to ignore his relationships and obligations to others unless reason dictated otherwise. Living the good life meant embracing the life you were living, seeing the majesty of the life you were given rather than running away from it. No wonder he taught in a public marketplace, pacing up and down the Colonnade as his audience listened.

Although the young Zeno was quite influenced by Cynicism, he did not teach Cynicism in its purest form. He took the basic ideas of Cynicism and combined them with what he learned from other schools of philosophy. People didn't know what to call it. For a while, they called it Zenonism.

Zeno attracted many creative students. One of his students, Ariston of Chios, introduced one of the important concepts of Stoicism: the doctrine of indifference. He suggested we should live in a state of indifference with respect to things that are between virtue and vice. Just as an actor is indifferent to the type of role he or she plays, we should be indifferent to events that cannot be considered virtues or vices. He was attracted to the Stoic doctrine that wise persons are not dogmatic in their view of the world. Another of his students, Cleanthes, succeeded him as the head of Stoa.

Softening Cynicism

As he went on, Zeno started to give up the harsher aspects of Cynicism. He retained the idea of living according to nature but deemphasized the ascetic aspects of Cynicism. He didn't think it was necessary to give up the good things in life, beg for food, be shameless, or live in a barrel. He did not ask his followers to practice asceticism, reject social conventions, or stop enjoying the good things in life.

Zeno also deviated from Cynicism by saying things that are morally indifferent (those things not totally under our control) can still have value if they contributed to the instinct of self-preservation. He started the process of making philosophy more and more pragmatic, a process that continued for several centuries after him.

A kinder and gentler version of Cynicism was thus born.

Zeno was an orator, not a writer. What little he wrote was reputed to be written poorly and, in any case, his writings were lost. He was widely respected because he was seen as friendly, unassuming, and dignified.

> *Stoicism according to Zeno*
>
> *The goal of Stoicism is to "live consistently." One should lead a life of reason because reason is the only thing that is consistent with itself. A consistent life leads to happiness.*
>
> *There are three aspects to Stoicism:*
> *Physics: What is the nature of things?*
> *Logic: How to apply reason to our thinking*
> *Ethics: How to develop character*
>
> *A life lived according to reason is a virtuous life because it enables life to flow evenly, resulting in happiness. Vice is a rejection of reason. Therefore, vice and virtue cannot coexist.*
>
> *Things are good, bad, or indifferent. The good belong to virtue; the bad belong to vice. All other things are indifferent. Indifferent things include everything that we don't fully control such as "life and death, beauty and ugliness, strengths and weaknesses, honor"[5] etc.*
>
> *Indifferent things can nevertheless have value. The value of indifferent things is proportional to how they aid self-preservation. For example, health aids self-preservation. So it has value even though it is morally indifferent.*
>
> *There are four negative emotions: desire, fear, pleasure, and pain. There are three positive emotions: will, caution, and joy.*

Zeno was so popular the Athenians offered him citizenship. Even though he loved Athens and adopted it as his city, living there for more than 50 years, Zeno still identified himself with his birth city of Citium and turned down the offer.

Zeno continued to develop his philosophy to include logic, especially the kind developed by the Dialectical School. He defined happiness as the smooth flow of life and was then joined by others. People started referring to his philosophy as the philosophy of the stoa (porch) or Stoicism. Zenonism wasn't a catchy name anyway.

A fortunate storm

Three unconnected events – a play in Thebes, a misanthrope exiled for debasing the currency in Sinope, and a shipwreck in Piraeus – gave rise to circumstances that bought three unlikely characters (Crates, Diogenes, and Zeno) together in Athens and eventually contributed in different degrees to the birth of the Stoic philosophy. An improbable story indeed.

The birth of Stoicism owes its existence to a fortunate storm 2,300 years ago. But for that storm, you wouldn't be reading this book.

The strange story continues.

Notes

[1] Inwood, Brad and Gerson, Lloyd P. (2008) *The Stoics Reader.* Hackett Publishing Company.

[2] The 3rd century CE writer Diogenes Laertius, who wrote on the lives of many Greek philosophers

[3] Kidd 2005, Long 1996, (Wikipedia Cynicism)

[4] Wikipedia, *Diogenes of Sinope*

[5] Stock, George. *A Little Book of Stoicism.* Ten Cent Pocket Series. (Available on Amazon.)

CHAPTER 2

The Story of the Seven Scholarchs

Five hundred years of Stoic thought

The school that Zeno founded flourished for about five centuries, until the death of its most famous practitioner, Emperor Marcus Aurelius, in the year 180 CE. When Stoicism started, there was a formal head (scholar or scholarch) of the school, starting with Zeno and continuing with six more scholarchs. They were followed by some of the best-known Stoics who were not scholarchs.

The first three scholarchs – Zeno of Citium, Cleanthes, and Chrysippus – are considered the founders of Stoicism. Four more scholarchs (Zeno of Tarsus, Diogenes, Antipater, and Penaetius) followed them. These seven cover the early and the middle stoa. This chapter tells the story of these seven scholarchs who taught Stoicism between 300 BCE to approximately the birth of Christ.

The Stoic periods and the great Stoics

Scholars divide the development of Stoic thinking into three distinct periods. The following were the heads (scholarchs) of Stoicism:

EARLY STOA

Zeno of Citium

Cleanthes of Assos

Chrysippus of Soli

Zeno of Tarsus

Diogenes of Babylon

Antipater of Tarsus

MIDDLE STOA

Panaetius of Rhodes

(Panaetius was the last scholarch, although other Stoics such as Posidonius taught Stoicism during this period.)

LATE STOA

Great Stoics during this period included the following.

Musonius Rufus

Seneca

Epictetus

Marcus Aurelius

> NOTE. *In ancient Greece, people were referred to by a single name like Zeno or Cleanthes. However, they were many prominent people (such as Zeno and Diogenes) with the same name. To avoid confusion, people added the native city of a person to the name (Zeno of Elea, Zeno of Citium, Zeno of Tarsus, etc.)*

Zeno to God: Why do you call me?

We already met Zeno of Citium, the first head of Stoicism. He became familiar to Athenians as the philosopher who would walk up and down the painted colonnade, to keep the colonnade clear of idle onlookers. Athenians held him in high esteem. They honored him by depositing with him the keys of the city walls. They also gave him a golden crown and erected a bronze statue in his image.

Not to be outdone, his native city of Citium also erected a bronze statue in his honor. Antigonus of Gontas, the powerful ruler of Macedon, came to listen to Zeno whenever he came to Athens. Antigonus often invited Zeno to come to the ruler's court. Zeno declined and sent two of his students instead.

All in all, Zeno was well-respected, honored, and provided for during his lifetime, something that cannot be said of many philosophers who followed him. Although he had many followers, he named his student of nineteen years, Cleanthes, as the next scholarch.

One day when Zeno was leaving his school, he stumbled and broke his toe. As he fell to the ground, he addressed the gods, saying "Why do you call me?"

He died immediately, at the age of seventy-two, although some claim[1] he was ninety-eight.

Cleanthes: The boxer takes over

Cleanthes of Assos, chosen by Zeno to head the Stoics, was a boxer by profession. He was poor and arrived in Athens with four drachmas. He met Zeno and started studying philosophy with him. Cleanthes not only absorbed Zeno's teachings, he adhered to them throughout his life.

Philosopher by day, gardener by night

He wrote down Zeno's lectures on oyster shells and blade bones of oxen because he was too poor to buy something to write on. Cleanthes spent all day studying philosophy. Being poor, to earn money, he watered gardens at night.

When people noticed he attended school all day even though he was poor, they hauled him to court to explain how he supported himself and paid for his tuition. In defense, he produced as witnesses the gardener whose garden he watered and the women who sold the meal which he used to crush to earn money.

Moved by his story, Antigonus made him a present of three thousand drachmas and the court voted for a donation of ten minas, which Zeno forbade Cleanthes to accept.

The likable dullard

Cleanthes was diligent but very slow. One of his contemporaries said of the philosopher:

"Who is this that, like a bell-weather ranges over the ranks of men, a dullard, lover of verse, hailing from Assos, a mass of rock, unventuresome?"[2]

When people taunted him and called him a donkey, he simply responded they were correct; only he was strong enough to carry the load for Zeno. When reproached for his cowardice, he replied, "That's why I seldom go wrong."

When Cleanthes was criticized as slow-witted, Zeno defended him by comparing him to tablets of hard wax; they were hard to write on, but retained what was written.[3]

Cleanthes took nothing personally, and this endeared him to people. The poet Sositheus once mocked Cleanthes with this verse, "Driven by Cleanthes' folly like dumb herds." When the audience noticed Cleanthes was present in the theater and remained unmoved, they were astonished, applauded Cleanthes, and drove Sositheus off the stage.

People's admiration of Cleanthes increased further when they heard about this incident. Once, he was leading youths to a public spectacle. A sudden gust of wind blew his cloak away. They saw he was wearing no shirt, and they applauded his simplicity.[4]

Even Zeno, who charged Cleanthes for tuition and fined him when he was out of line, admired him. Once when Zeno was with a friend he produced a handful of small coins and said, "Cleanthes could even maintain a second Cleanthes, if he wished. Yet those who possess the means to keep themselves seek to live at the expense of others, even though they have plenty of time to spare from their studies."

Although Cleanthes was industrious and absorbed all the teachings of his master, he was extraordinarily slow. He had no aptitude for physics. Under his guidance, Stoicism remained stable but did not advance.

Among Cleanthes' students was the brilliant Chrysippus. He often challenged Cleanthes and yet even Chrysippus fell into remorse afterward and wrote these lines:

> *Blessed in all else I am*
>
> *Save only where I touch Cleanthes*
>
> *There I am ill-fortuned.*

When some dialectician attacked Cleanthes on logic, Chrysippus sprang to his defense and said, "Don't distract your elders from matters of importance. Leave such arguments to us juniors."

"The way has already been prepared for me."

The teachings of Cleanthes had a religious fervor. He said of evil,

> *Just as a boil that comes to a head is less dangerous than a tumor which does not, so evil deeds are less harmful than evil thoughts*[5].

As he aged, Cleanthes' gums became badly swollen. His doctors ordered him to abstain from food for two days, which he did. He got better, and the doctors allowed him to resume his regular diet. Instead, he continued to abstain from food, saying the way had already been prepared for him. He died of starvation died at 72, the same age his master Zeno is said to have died.

Chrysippus, the long-distance runner, follows

While he well understood the teachings of his master Zeno, Cleanthes did not have the intellectual heft to advance Stoicism any further. As likable as he was, Cleanthes was no exciting teacher. Under his leadership, Stoicism started losing students to rival schools and desperately needed a charismatic leader. That role was filled by Chrysippus of Soli, who became the third head of Stoicism, in around 230 BCE, when Cleanthes died.

Give me the principles and I will find the proof

Chrysippus (279 BCE – 206 BCE) was born in Soli to Apollonius of Tarsus. Slight in stature, he was trained as a long-distance runner.[6] He came from a wealthy family, and he inherited his father's property. Subsequently, the property was confiscated to the king's treasury.

> *If I had followed the crowd, I should not have studied philosophy.*
>
> Chrysippus

The freshly poor Chrysippus turned to philosophy for consolation. He began studying Stoicism. He was an outstanding student of Cleanthes and possibly Zeno as well. Confident personally and forceful intellectually, Chrysippus was reputed to have told Cleanthes, "Give me the principles, and I will find the proofs myself."

Chrysippus was a maverick. Once, when somebody reproached him for not going along with others to hear Ariston, Chrysippus replied, "If I had followed the crowd, I should not have studied philosophy."

If there were no Chrysippus, there would be no stoa

The life of Chrysippus was a busy one.[7] He spent most of his time lecturing and writing, often isolating himself from social engagements. Yet he fulfilled his duties to his family.

He excelled in many areas Stoics were interested in: theory of knowledge, ethics, physics, and especially logic. He created a system of propositional logic as opposed to Aristotle's term logic. He was so well known for his expertise in logic that when Clement of Alexandria wanted to identify the master among logicians (like Homer was among poets), he chose Chrysippus over Aristotle.[8] Advances in logic in the 20th Century in propositional calculus emphasized the importance of logical principles developed by Chrysippus. Diogenes Laertius commented,

> *If there were a dialectic among the gods, it would be none other than Chrysippus.*
>
> Diogenes Laertius[9]

Chrysippus was brilliant, and he knew he was. Nor was he hampered by a false sense of modesty.

Someone asked, "To whom should I send my son to study?"

"To me," replied Chrysippus, "for even if I dreamt there were anyone better than I, I would be philosophizing with him myself."

So it is said of him, "If there were no Chrysippus, there would be no stoa."

Chrysippus: The good and the questionable

While Cleanthes was still living, Chrysippus withdrew from his school and attained an exceptional reputation as an eminent philosopher. He was the first to deliver a class lecture in the open air in the Lyceum.

He was highly productive and methodical and composed more than 700 works, diligently writing 500 lines a day. Currently, none of his works survive except as quotes in the works of authors such as Cicero, Seneca, Galen, and Plutarch. Recently, segments from Logical Questions, On Providence, and a third work by Chrysippus were discovered among the Herculaneum papyri.[10]

In his writings, Chrysippus was not happy simply to present his side of arguments but would cite explanations by rival philosophers so he could refute them. His rivals accused him of filling his books with quotes from others. As Apollodorus of Athens sarcastically observed, "If one were to strip the books of Chrysippus of all extraneous quotations, his pages would be left bare."

Some of Chrysippus' writings contained controversial ideas. According to Diogenes Laertius in On the Republic and On Things Not Worth Choosing for Their Own Sakes, Chrysippus was reported to have said [one may] lie with mothers, daughters, and sons. In On the Just, he is reported to have said [people] should eat the dead.

The second founder of Stoicism

Chrysippus was highly respected and was seen as the authority on Stoicism although his style was considered obscure and careless. He polished the extant Stoic principles and extended

Stoic thought further. As a result, he was considered the "second founder of Stoicism."

Give the donkey a drink of wine

Chrysippus died when he was 73 – approximately the same age as Zeno and Cleanthes when they died. There are a couple of versions of how he died. A popular one says that Chrysippus was attending the 143rd Olympiad. While at the games he saw a donkey eat some figs. He found it so funny that he yelled, "Now give the donkey a drink of pure wine to wash down the figs." He found the situation so funny he died laughing.

Zeno, Cleanthes, and Chrysippus – the first three scholarchs of Stoicism are considered to be the founding fathers of Stoicism. Not much is known of the next four scholarchs, whose stories follow.

Zeno of Tarsus

When Chrysippus died around 206 BCE, Zeno of Tarsus, a pupil of Chrysippus, became the head of Stoicism. Zeno's father was Dioscorides, also a Stoic and a student of Chrysippus.

The fourth Stoic scholarch did not write very much so little is known of his views.[11] However, he had a great many students and through them, we know he was an orthodox Stoic, but did not believe in the doctrine of the conflagration of the universe.[12]

Until then, Stoic physics held that the Universe periodically dissolved into fire. While Zeno's diversion from this belief might have been a revolutionary idea at the time, it has very little bearing on core Stoic ideas, especially as we understand them today.

We don't know how Zeno of Tarsus died.

Diogenes of Babylon

When Zeno of Tarsus died, Diogenes of Babylon (230 BCE – 150/140 BCE) assumed the leadership of Stoicism as the fifth scholarch. Diogenes was born in Seleucia on the Tigris in Babylon and studied in Athens under Chrysippus. He closely followed the views of his teacher, especially on matters of logic.

Around 155 BCE, a fine of one hundred talents was imposed on Athens for the sack of Oropus. Diogenes, his pupil Carneades, and Critolaus, were sent to Rome to appeal the fine. They delivered speeches in numerous private assemblies, then in the Senate. Diogenes delighted his audience with his sober and temperate manner of speaking.[13]

Diogenes wrote several books. Unfortunately, we know only the names of those works, not their content. He did not just write about Stoicism; his works included topics such as On Music and On Rhetoric.[14] Cicero's writings indicate Diogenes also wrote about several other topics such as duty and the highest good.[15]

Cicero believed Diogenes was "a great and important Stoic."[16] Even the Epicurean philosopher Philodemus discussed Diogenes more often than any other philosopher, except for Epicurus.

According to Lucien,[17] Diogenes died when he was 80, while some believe he died at 70.

Antipater of Tarsus

Antipater of Tarsus, a pupil of Diogenes of Babylon, became the last scholarch of the early Stoa. As with most other early scholarchs, not much is known about his life either. We don't even know his birth year. What little we know of him comes from references to him found in other people's works.

Plutarch considered him as a principal Stoic figure, along with Zeno, Cleanthes, and Chrysippus.[18]

Cicero refers to Antipater's remarkable "acuteness."[19]

Antipater, the "Pen-noise"

During his leadership, he participated in many debates between Stoicism and Plato's rival school, Academy. However, Antipater concluded he was so unequal in public arguments to his contemporary Carneades, he would confine himself to writing, which earned him the name "Pen-noise."[20]

The dilemma of the wise man and the counterfeit money

Antipater believed Fate was a god, and Gods were good and incorruptible. He wrote on moral philosophy and created a work called On Superstition. Because his writings did not survive all we can gather from scattered references to his work is he took "higher ground" in solving moral dilemmas than his master Diogenes of Babylon.[21] Here are some examples:

> *A wise man unknowingly accepts counterfeit money and then discovers his mistake. Should he use this money when he needs to repay a debt? Yes, says Diogenes; no, says Antipater.*
> *A store owner knows his wine is spoilt. Should he tell his customers? No, says Diogenes; yes, says Antipater.*[22]

Antipater died around 130 BCE.

Panaetius of Rhodes, the last scholarch

Panaetius of Rhodes (c. 185 – c. 110 BCE) was the seventh and last undisputed scholarch of Stoicism. He studied under the previous two scholarchs: Diogenes of Babylon and Antipater of Tarsus.

Panaetius introduced Greek philosophy, especially Stoicism, to Rome. By doing this, he influenced the course of Stoic history. While in Rome, he attracted many star disciples such as Quintus Aelius Tubero.

Panaetius was born into an eminent Rhodian family. He moved to Athens and studied with several philosophers but chose Stoicism as his principal focus. He was so well respected that, around 149 BCE, he was chosen by the people of Lindos on Rhodes to be the priest of Poseidon Hippios. [23]

Panaetius resided mainly in Athens although from time to time he also lived in Rome. When he succeeded Antipater of Tarsus as head of the Stoic school, he was offered citizenship by the Athenians, but he declined it. He died in Athens sometime around 110 BCE.

The contribution of Panaetius to Stoic philosophy is the most eclectic of the scholarchs. He modified Stoic doctrines to suit his aristocratic disciples and maintained it was not necessary to be a perfect sage to be happy.[24] Because of his eclectic thinking, even the Neoplatonists considered him one of their own.[25]

In shaping the Stoic doctrines, he believed Physics was more important than Logic. He did not believe in the Stoic doctrine of the conflagration of the universe. While he held that virtues are inseparable, he recognized two forms of virtue, the theoretical and the practical. He argued that moral definitions should be proposed in a manner that made it easy for people who have not attained wisdom to understand and apply.[26] He wrote On Duties, a book in three volumes, none of which survive today.

Seven scholarchs of Stoicism. The first three founded Stoicism while the last one exported it to Rome. And the three scholarchs in between, we know very little about. Almost none of their work, except Cleanthes' Hymn, survives today. What we know of their Stoicism comes to us in the form of quotes and brief summaries in other books. Stoicism, as we know it today, is based almost entirely on late Stoa.

Before we move on to late Stoa, let's look at some prominent non-Stoic influence on Stoicism.

Non-Stoic heroes of Stoicism

Stoics were not averse to taking good ideas from wherever they came. Epicureanism was a direct rival of Stoicism, and yet Stoics did not hesitate to quote Epicurus in their writings.

We also noted how the Stoic doctrines were based on the ideas developed by Diogenes of Sinope, a Cynic. Diogenes provided the intellectual framework for Stoicism to flourish.

If Diogenes was the intellectual father of Stoicism, Socrates was its wise godfather.

Socrates as a *de facto* sage

Stoics asked the question whether it was possible for us to become ideal humans by being virtuous, living in accordance with nature. They did not answer the question directly, but they conceived of someone who had so attained the ideal. This person, in Stoic literature, is called a sage.

Stoics often talked about the sage as their role model. When they referred to sage-like qualities in a human being, they referred most frequently to Socrates, even though Socrates had been dead for more than sixty years before the founder of Stoicism was even born. It was a full century after the death of Socrates when Stoicism was conceived.

So how did Socrates become a *de facto* sage who Stoics admired so much? Stripped of its "physics" and references to supernatural entities, Stoicism is nothing more than a logical argument of how things work and how one can get the best out of life by aligning one's thinking with the way things work. Consequently, it is possible for people to come to the same conclusions as a Stoic without ever having been exposed to Stoicism.[27]

Like the Stoics, Socrates let ethics guide his life. Both used logic to guide their decisions. Socrates was ugly-looking, and yet he was not hindered by it; known instead for his intellect.[28] As the Stoics contended, the state of your body is no hindrance to your mind.

Like the Stoics, Socrates cultivated his body but did not give primacy to it. His challenging of conventions and stressing of a simple way of life echoed the Stoic approach.

Finally, when he was sentenced to die, Socrates did not flee or complain but accepted his fate, just as a Stoic would. Thus Socrates became a real-life sage for the Stoics (although they never acknowledged this), approaching the Stoic ideal.

Cicero, the polymath

Marcus Tullius Cicero (106 – 43 BCE) was a polymath: an orator, lawyer, politician, and philosopher. He considered politics to be above philosophy, and he wrote on philosophical matters only when he was prevented from taking part in politics.[29] His political life included many political actions and, following the death of Julius Caesar, his enmity to Mark Anthony. As a result, Mark Anthony had Cicero murdered. His life was a really fascinating one, but here we will we confine ourselves to his relevance to Stoicism.

Neither Cicero nor others considered him a Stoic. In fact, Cicero was often critical of Stoicism. While Cicero professed allegiance to First Academy, he summarized in Latin the doctrines of different Greek philosophical schools including Stoicism, Skepticism, Peripateticism, and Epicureanism. He was well acquainted with all these schools of philosophy.

Because of his preference for action in political matters, Cicero turned to Stoicism which advocated it. According to Stoicism, we are all part of humanity, and we all share human laws. Therefore, we have a duty to participate in humanity's welfare, including taking political action when warranted. Stoics sought the betterment of the community, and not power or money, which they held as meaningless.

While Cicero wrote critically about Stoicism and Stoic thought, he selectively accepted Stoic principles and ideas. His writings on Stoicism are an important source of Stoic thought prevalent just before the late Stoa. He laid out six Stoic principles he called "paradoxes" which an average person would find difficult to understand and probably disagree with.

SIX STOIC PARADOXES

Moral worth is the only good.

Virtue is sufficient for happiness.

All sins and virtues are equal.

Every fool is insane.

Only the wise person is really free.

Only the wise person is really rich.

After laying out the paradoxes, Cicero then proceeded to demonstrate their validity.

Unlike the works of the early Stoics, Cicero's work has been preserved and provides an outline of Stoic thought when it was still centered in Athens rather than in Rome. He was, along with Panaetius, an early popularizer of Stoic thought in Rome. Because of his popularizing of Stoicism, and because he was often sympathetic to Stoic doctrines, Cicero is frequently referred to in Stoic literature.

Stoicism moves to Rome

The seventh scholarch, Panaetius, and Cicero were instrumental in introducing Romans to Stoicism. Rome was receptive to the idea of Stoicism (with some modifications), and Stoic leadership moved from Athens to Rome by about the time of Jesus Christ. Roman Stoicism did not have formal leaders but had four recognizable thought leaders, whose stories are next.

Notes

[1] Inwood, Brad and Gerson, Lloyd P. (2008) *The Stoics Reader*. Hackett Publishing Company.

[2] Attributed to Timor in *The Stoics* by Diogenes Laertius.

[3] Inwood, Brad and Gerson, Lloyd P. (2008) *The Stoics Reader*. Hackett Publishing Company.

[4] Demetrius of Meganasia *Men of the Same Name*. Quoted by Diogenes Laertius.

[5] Hadas, Moses, Ed. (1961) *Essential Works of Stoicism*. Bantam Books.

[6] Diogenes Laertius. *Lives and Opinions of Eminent Philosophers*.

[7] Gould, J.B. (1970) *The Philosophy of Chrysippus*. SUNYPress, New York: NY.

[8] Wikipedia Chrysippus retrieved April 29, 2016.

[9] Inwood, Brad and Gerson, Lloyd P. (2008) *The Stoics Reader*. Hackett Publishing Company.

[10] The first of Chrysippus' partially preserved two or three works is his *Logical Questions*, contained in PHerc. 307 ... The second work is his *On Providence*, preserved in PHerc 1038 and 1421 ... A third work, most likely by Chrysippus is preserved in PHerc. 1020," Fitzgerald 2004, p. 11

[11] Diogenes Laertius *Lives and Opinions of Eminent Philosophers*.

[12] Eusebius, *Praeparatio Evangelica*. (as referred to in Wikipedia entry of Zeno of Tarsus, August 30, 2016)

[13] Aulus Gellius. *Attic Nights*; Cicero *Academia* (Quoted in Wikipedia, 30/8/16)

[14] Easterling, P.E., and Knox, Bernard (1989) *The Cambridge History of Hellenistic Philosophy*. Cambridge University Press.

[15] Cicero *De Officiis*

[16] Cicero *De Officiis*

[17] Lucien *Mcrobii*
[18] Plutarch de Stoic. *Repugnant*. (Referred to in Wikipedia entry on Antipater.)
[19] Cicero *De Officiis*
[20] Plutach Moralia: *On Talkativness*; Eusebius, *Perparatio Evangelica*, ix.8 (Reference from Wikipedia)
[21] Wikipedia. Antipater of Tarsus
[22] Cicero *De Officiis, iii*
[23] Easterling, P.E., and Knox, Bernard (1989) *The Cambridge History of Hellenistic Philosophy*. Cambridge University Press.
[24] Hadas, Moses. Ed. (1961) *Essential Works of Stoicism*. Bantam Books.
[25] Proclus in *Plat. Tim.* (Wikipedia)
[26] Seneca, *Epistles*, 116. 5
[27] As an example, in my book *Unshakable Freedom*, I quote sixteen-year-old Malala Yousufzai who's unlikely to have read any Stoic writing. (She was actually fighting with terrorists for her right to go to school.) And yet what she said about terrorists could have been said by a wise Stoic. Stoic attitudes are not uncommon among those who have never been exposed to Stoicism.
[28] Morrison, D.R. (2011) *The Cambridge Companion to Socrates* (*p.xiv*). Cambridge University Press, *ISBN 0521833426.* Retrieved *2015-04-16*; Nails, D. *Socrates: Socrates' Strangeness* The Stanford Encyclopedia of Philosophy (Spring 2014 Edition), Edward N. Zalta (ed.). Retrieved *2015-04-16*.
[29] *Internet Encyclopedia of Philosophy*, entry on Cicero

CHAPTER 3

The Story of a Slave and an Emperor (and Two Others)

Almost everything we know firsthand about Stoicism has its origins in Rome. Unlike Athenian Stoicism, Roman Stoicism had no formal heads or scholarchs. Instead, without formal leadership, it produced Stoics who wrote and taught for nearly two hundred years.

Four major figures stand out from this period: Seneca, Rufus, Epictetus, and Aurelius. Their stories are no less strange than those of the early Stoics. They were, like the early Stoics, vastly different in their backgrounds and led colorful lives. While we still don't know everything about their lives, we know more about them than the early scholarchs, and, more importantly, a large body of their work survives.

Seneca, the exile who tutored an emperor

In 4 BCE, a child was born in Cordoba, Spain, who turned out to be probably the most lucid writer on Roman Stoicism. His name was Lucius Annaeus Seneca (4 BCE – 65 CE), also known as Seneca the Younger. Although his father, Seneca the Elder, was also a Stoic, the Younger learned Stoicism under Attalus. Seneca, born into a rich and powerful Iberian family, was not just a Stoic philosopher, he was also a Roman statesman, banker, poet, and dramatist, known for his tragedies.

Few today are likely to experience the ups and downs of Seneca's life. Rich as he was, he was sickly. He suffered from asthma and was heavily depressed. After his education in Rome, he stayed there to pursue a career in government and came close to the seat of power. He came to the attention of Emperor Caligula. That turned out to be a double-edged sword. When Seneca made a powerful speech that was widely applauded, Emperor Caligula became jealous. He spared Seneca's life only because he believed Seneca would die soon.[1]

The reprieve did not last long. Messalina, the wife of the next Emperor Claudius, accused Seneca of committing adultery with the Emperor's niece, Julia Livilla, and had him banished in 41 CE.

Banishment was hard on Seneca. Corsica was a barren and thorny rock, an uncivilized and inhospitable island. No one there spoke or understood Latin. Seneca took comfort in Stoic doctrines and wrote to his mother consoling her. He said he was always prepared to give up his material goods at a moment's notice, and banishment is nothing more than living in a different place. What's so bad about that?[2]

While in exile, Seneca continued to plead his case for restoration, some say, unlike a real Stoic. In 49 CE, eight years after his exile, he was allowed to return to Rome. At the behest of the then Emperor Claudius' wife, Agrippina, he became a tutor to the future Emperor Nero. Thus Seneca was back to his affluent life after enduring a miserable eight years. He became the most renowned citizen of Rome, a well-recognized writer of prose and poetry, as well as the favorite of the Empress Agrippina.

After Nero became emperor, Seneca continued as his advisor. Nero learned nothing of Seneca's Stoic principles and didn't care for them either. Just the opposite. He was cruel, arbitrary, by any standards evil and bizarre.

For five years, Seneca kept Nero's evil tendencies in check, but the philosopher gradually lost his grip on the emperor. Nero accused Seneca of having inappropriate relations with his mother. He ordered many people killed on a whim, even his own mother (who was no angel herself, having ordered many people who stood in her way killed[3], including her own husband Claudius, so Nero could come to power). Nero even involved Seneca in his evil deeds, forcing him to plot the murder of Nero's mother and justify it to the Senate.[4] It would appear it was Nero who ended up having a hold on Seneca rather than the other way around.

Some modern philosophers consider Seneca a hypocrite while others argue that, without Seneca's influence, Nero would have been even more evil.[5] Seneca's extravagant lifestyle was incompatible with our modern image of Stoicism, although Stoicism considers wealth a matter of indifference. We also should remember much of Seneca's image as a hypocrite comes from a single source: Sullius, his unrelenting critic.

Irrespective of whether Seneca was a hypocrite or not, his exposition of the Stoic principles applied in different contexts is among the most elegant writings of Stoicism. His writings continue to inspire people to lead a more productive life to this day.[6] A more generous interpretation of Seneca's actions would be that he was a man forced to face impossible moral dilemmas who did the best he could.

His legacy includes a dozen philosophical essays, 124 letters dealing with moral issues, and epistles ("longer" letters) now called *Epistulae morales ad Lucilium*. The letters were written to his friend Lucilius, who had an Epicurean inclination. These letters were a veiled attempt to win him over to Stoicism. Most of them were written towards the end of Seneca's life, between 63 and 65 CE.

The wealthy Stoic

While serving Nero, Seneca became very wealthy and led an opulent life. He became a money lender and built a fortune, estimated at more than 300 million sestertii, making him a multimillionaire by today's standards. He also owned several villas and vineyards around Italy. He lived in luxury, owning 500 identical citrus-wood tables with ivory legs that he used when he threw lavish dinner parties to entertain 1,000 of his closest friends.

It was quite likely, in spite of what his position brought him in terms of wealth and power, that Seneca wanted out. He requested Nero to relieve him of his responsibilities several times, but the Emperor refused.

Seneca tried again when he was 66, pleading his case as an old man who just wanted to retire. This time, Nero relented. Seneca packed his bags and quietly retired to his country estates (a far cry from his exile in Corsica), seldom visiting Rome. But his retirement did not last too long. Three years later, when he was 69 years old, Nero accused, rather dubiously, Seneca of being involved in the abortive Pisonian conspiracy to kill the emperor.[7] He ordered Seneca to kill himself. Seneca had no choice.

The end of Seneca

Seneca's death was neither quick nor pretty. He first tried to end his life instantly by slitting his wrist. But his age worked against him. He was bleeding too slowly to die. He tried cutting his arteries in his legs and knees, but he remained alive.

Then he drank poison. That did not work either.

Finally, his friends carried him to a bathtub so he could fill the room with steam and suffocate.[8]

Thus died one of the most unusual figures of Stoicism. In turn, rich, exiled, ultra-rich, and famous, Seneca died like a Stoic and admonished his friends who were present not to mourn his death.

Rufus, the third founder of Stoicism

While the controversy about Seneca played out, another man, Gaius Musonius Rufus (30 – 100 CE) ran the first official school of Stoicism in Rome. The least known of the four famous Stoics of the late Stoa, his claim to historical fame is mostly as the teacher of Epictetus. By his contemporaries, he was considered the Roman Socrates and the third founder of Stoicism.[9]

Musonius Rufus, by birth an Etruscan, was a Roman knight. Rather than using his influential family's position to get ahead in politics, he chose to pursue Stoic philosophy. He declared, among other things, that it was all right to disobey unjust laws. This position earned him banishment to an island by Nero and, at a later date, by Vespasian.

While practically none of Musonius' works survived, his pupil Lucius took notes during his lectures in which Lucius wrote about what Musonius said when he was asked a question. We also have quotes attributed to Musonius by Epictetus, Musonius' star student.

Considered as the most pragmatic of all Roman Stoics, Rufus offered solutions to everyday problems of living. Like all Stoics, he thought we should be involved in the affairs of the world and not withdraw from it like Epicureans suggested.

While he held homosexuality and abortion as contrary to nature, he advocated women's rights. He was for civic duty, charity, education, free speech, forgiveness, pacifism, and brotherly love. He also held things like gladiatorial fights and recreational sex as immoral.

As far as daily life was concerned, Rufus advocated simplicity and avoidance of excesses. He held that the purpose of clothing and footwear was not to attract the attention of others but to provide protection from the elements, and there was no need to go beyond modest, simple, and inexpensive items. Even total protection from the elements was to be avoided. A little discomfort was good.

Similarly, the home should be designed to be functional rather than showy. Instead of spending money excessively, one should use it to help others. Rufus believed pursuing luxurious things fostered injustice and greed, and mistaking them for good things was like an insane person mistaking black for white.

Musonius' teachings are hardly read or practiced these days. However, the same cannot be said of Epictetus, his most famous disciple.

Epictetus, philosophy's most famous slave

We know Epictetus as one of the most important and widely read Stoic philosophers of all time. His writings (as transcribed by his disciple, Arrian) provide the only existing framework for understanding Stoic philosophy.

But who was Epictetus? We don't even know his name, although we know he was a slave. "Epictetus" simply means "acquired." Was that his real name? If not, what was his real name? Did he even have a name? We don't know.

Epictetus was born c. 55 CE in Hierapolis (present day Pamukkale, Turkey). It is said his parents sold him to Epaphroditos, a wealthy freedman, and secretary to Nero. But how did his parents get to Rome to make the sale happen? We don't know.

We know Epictetus was lame. But how did he become lame? We don't know that for sure either. According to some accounts, Epaphroditos broke both Epictetus' legs for no reason. Other accounts say Epictetus' legs were broken by a previous master. There is even an account which says his lameness was due to rheumatism.

In any case, the lame Epictetus spent his youth as a slave in Rome. Even as a slave, Epictetus was found to be gifted. Epaphroditos sent him to study with Musonius Rufus. It might sound illogical that the slave master who is reputed to have had Epictetus' legs broken would send him to study philosophy. However, it was not unusual for a slave master to brag about his slaves being philosophers or masters of some other subject.

Eventually, Epictetus became a free man, but again we don't know exactly how. After he had gained his freedom, Epictetus began to teach his philosophy. But not for long.

Around 93 CE, Emperor Domitian banished all philosophers from Rome. Epictetus fled to Nicopolis in Greece where he founded his philosophy school and remained until his death around 135 CE. Epictetus was luckier than his former master Epaphroditus, who was put to death by Domitian two years later.

As far as we know, Epictetus had never married and never had any children. But like all Stoics, he encouraged people to be involved in life. He encouraged others to get married and have children. In his old age, he adopted a child of his friend who would otherwise be left to die. He also enlisted the help of a woman to raise the child.[10] He was so respected that, when he died, one of his admirers bought his lamp for 3,000 drachmae.[11]

Although he left no writings of his own, his disciple Flavius Arrian faithfully transcribed the teachings of Epictetus. He collected them into eight books called Discourses, only four of which survive today. Also, Arrian captured a summary of Epictetus' teaching in a small manual called Enchiridion (Handbook).

Aurelius, the Emperor inspired by a slave

Marcus Aurelius was born in Rome in 121 CE into a wealthy and politically prominent family. He was a dedicated student of Latin and Greek. His teacher, Junius Rusticus, introduced him to the teachings of Epictetus which had a great deal of influence on the young Marcus.

Marcus Aurelius was unique among famous Stoics. He was neither poor, exiled, murdered, nor forced to commit suicide. Quite the contrary. He was the Emperor of Rome.

And what an empire it was! It was one of the largest empires the world had ever seen. The empire stretched from Hadrian's Wall in England to the banks of the Euphrates in Syria; it included countries along the Rhine-Danube river system in Europe; from the Black Sea to Egypt, encompassing the entire Mediterranean.[12]

In fact, Marcus Aurelius was the most powerful man on earth at the time. Men of such power and influence, with arbitrary and unlimited power are seldom introspective, let alone turn to philosophy. But Aurelius did, to the great benefit of future generations.

While Aurelius was still in his early teens (14 to be exact), Epictetus died in Greece. Although many modern writers seem to assume Aurelius was a student[13] of Epictetus, there is no record of the two ever meeting.

As our strange story continues, the powerless lame exile, a man the Emperor is unlikely to have ever met, provided inspiration to the most powerful man on earth through his teachings.

How Marcus became an emperor

How Marcus Aurelius came to be an Emperor was in itself an interesting story. When Marcus was 15 years of age, Emperor Hadrian fell ill and nearly died. Realizing he might die soon, Hadrian designated a distinguished aristocrat Lucius Ceionius as the next Emperor. But Ceionius himself died the following year.

Hadrian then chose as his successor the childless Senator Pius Antoninus and asked him to adopt Marcus Aurelius along with Ceionius' son Lucius Verus. Around the age of 17, Marcus

Aurelius became the son of Antoninus, becoming Marcus Aurelius Antoninus. Hadrian died in 138 CE, and Pius Antoninus became the emperor. Marcus worked alongside his adopted father, learning the ways of government and public affairs.

In 140, Aurelius became Consul, the leader of the Senate. Over the years, he received more powers and responsibilities, and became a strong source of counsel for Antoninus. He married Faustina, the emperor's daughter, in 145 and had many children. After his adoptive father died in 161, Aurelius became the Emperor.

The troubled life of Marcus Aurelius

Unfortunately for Aurelius, his tenure was marked by war, treachery, and disease. He battled with the Parthian empire for control over lands in the East. Returning soldiers brought some type of disease back with them to Rome, which lingered for years and wiped out an estimated five million.[14]

After the Parthian War had ended, Aurelius faced military conflict with German tribes that crossed the Danube River and attacked a Roman city. Aurelius and his brother Verus fought the invaders.

Marcus' personal life did not go well either. His wife was not faithful to him (although most likely he didn't know) and even plotted against him. His son Commodus turned out to be a disappointment.

Verus died in 169, so Aurelius assumed the full responsibility for the battle. In 175, after hearing a rumor about Aurelius being deathly ill, Avidius Cassius proclaimed himself Emperor. As Aurelius traveled to the East to regain control, Cassius was murdered by his soldiers. Subsequently, Aurelius toured the eastern provinces with his wife who died during this time. Marcus Aurelius died in 180.

Meditations, the most widely read book on Stoicism

While he was away in battles, Marcus Aurelius kept a personal diary, commonly known as "To Himself" or "Meditations." Not meant for publication, the journal contained the Emperor's Stoic musings written under difficult circumstances. Fortunately for us, it was found and later published. It contains some of the finest writings on Stoicism written by a practitioner.

It is ironic that while most Stoic writings meant for public consumption disappeared over time, Marcus Aurelius' Meditations, clearly a personal journal not meant to be read by anyone else, became the most widely read work of Stoicism of all time.

Marcus Aurelius was the last great Stoic. After his death, it is likely Stoicim was practiced but there was no one who advanced the philosophy any further.

Notes

[1] Evan, Jules (2012) *Philosophy for Life and Other Dangerous Situations*. New World Library.

[2] Seneca. *Consolations to Helvia*

[3] According to "gossipy historian" Suetonius, referred to in Schoch's *The Secrets of Happiness*.

[4] Schoch, R. (2006) *The Secrets of Happiness*, Scriber.

[5] There are several modern references to Seneca's character.

[6] Chakrapani, Chuck (2016) *Unshakable Freedom*. The Stoic Gym.

[7] Hadas, Moses. Ed. (1961) *Essential Works of Stoicism*. Bantam Books.

[8] Tacitus 15, 62-64

[9] Gould, J.B. (1970) *The Philosophy of Chrysippus*. State University of NY Press, New York, NY.

[10] Simplicus. *Commentary on the Enchiridion*. (Source Wiki)

[11] Lucian, Remarks to an illiterate book-lover. (source Wiki

[12] Kelly, Christopher (2007) *Roman Empire: A very short Introduction*. OUP.

[13] Unless they mean it in a broad sense meaning Aurelius studied the philosophical thoughts of Epictetues.

[14] http://news.bbc.co.uk/2/hi/health/4381924.stm (Retrieved September 6, 2016).

CHAPTER 4

The Story of the Survival of Stoic Works

We live in the age of the Internet. And the Internet is a super-efficient copy machine. An obscure person may write a blog, and potentially thousands of copies are created instantly. Even before the age of the Internet, computers, copy machines, and printing presses made mass duplication of any written material easy.

But Stoics lived long before the time of printing presses. So it is not surprising that an estimated 99% of their works have disappeared. For example, Chrysippus alone was reputed to have written 705 works, none of which survived except their titles. What survived? Approximately one thousand pages of Stoic literature mostly written by Epictetus (via Arrian), Seneca, and Marcus Aurelius.

To make things worse, Emperor Justinian closed the Athenian Academy in 529 CE, and that was the end of many philosophic schools of thought, including Stoicism. The professors who taught at the Academy left the Byzantine Empire and moved to Persia, where the Shah is supposed to have welcomed them. With that, the last intellectual light was put out in Europe before it plunged into the Dark Ages.

Some Stoic texts did make it to the 21st Century. To understand how precarious the journey was, let's follow just one text, *Meditations*, by Marcus Aurelius.

Meditations is not the title Marcus Aurelius assigned to his writing. Most likely his work did not have a title, given that it was a notebook of personal reflections.

Upon his death in 180 CE, perhaps a family member, friend or an admirer saved it.[1] It is unclear whether it was copied and published at that time. Two centuries later several historians referred to Aurelius' "exhortations", without having access to the original work itself.[2] When Justinian banned all pagan philosophies in 529 CE, *Meditations* completely disappeared from public view.

Around 900 CE, Arethas Caesarea, a Byzantine scholar found the manuscript, *Meditations*. He loved it and so copied it and began mentioning it in his letters and works. His references implied that the existence of *Meditations* was commonly known to Byzantine scholars.

In 907 CE, Arethas wrote to Demetrius, Metropolitan of Heraclea, to say he (Arethas) had a copy of *Meditations* in poor shape which he recopied, so it could be passed to future generations in its renewed condition.

Not much is known about the fate of *Meditations* for the next four centuries. Around 1300 CE, quotes from *Meditations* started to appear in different sources.

The oldest manuscript currently available is with the Vatican Library, Vaticanus Graecus 1950. In the West, *Meditations* was not quoted until the 16th Century.

In 1559, Xylander (Wilhelm Holzmann) translated *Meditations* into Latin and published it with the now-lost manuscript. This is the only surviving copy of the work besides the Vaticanus Graecus, which dated back to the fourteenth Century.[3] It is quite obvious that if these two copies had been lost anytime over the next several years, we would not have had access to this most-read Stoic text.

Given the original was written in Koine Greek and was copied and recopied, travelling over the centuries, we can't even be sure how faithful the current versions are to the original manuscript. It is not clear whether the original manuscript was neatly divided into 12 chapters ("books"), and whether even the original sequence was preserved. Even when sources and sequences are agreed upon, English translations of the same passage can vary widely. Here is a random example:

> "Consider the past; such great changes of political supremacies. You may also foresee things which will be. For they will certainly be of like form, and it is not possible that they should deviate from the order of things which take place now." (Hadas[4])
>
> "Look at the past – empire succeeding empire – and from that, extrapolate the future: the same thing. No escape from the rhythm of events." (Hayes[5])

Both are translations of the same passage in Book 7.49 and express the same underlying meaning. Yet the way the meaning is expressed and the imageries evoked are quite different. Which version is more faithful to the original?

Now we can appreciate the tortuous route Meditations took to reach the modern reader, and the difficulty 21st Century scholars face in interpreting an ancient dialect. It doesn't end there; we are still faced with the problem of the same words assuming different meanings over time. We can only be grateful the gifts of the Stoics (at least enough of them) have reached us in some form, even if they are somewhat detached from the original.

Notes

[1] Hadot, Pierre (1998) *Inner Citadel*. Harvard.
[2] Eg. Historia Augusta, referred to by Hadot (1998) above.
[3] The history of *Meditations* described here has been based on two sources: Pierre Hadot (1998) above and Marcel van Ackeren. *A Companion to Marcus Aurelius* (2012).
[4] Hadas, Moses. Ed & Tr (1961) *Essential Works of Stoicism*. Bantam Books.
[5] Marcus Aurelius (2002) *Meditations* Translated by Gregory Hayes. The Modern Library.

EPILOG

How I Came to Write This Book

During the golden era of philosophy, about 2,500 years ago, many schools flourished in Greece and Rome. Cynicism, Epicureanism, Pythagoreanism, Peripateticism, the Academy (Plato), Skepticism, just to name a few. Of all these schools, only one survived mainly in the form it was conceived: Stoicism. It's a philosophy of life that has interested me since my teens, when I stumbled upon it in the library.

I was intrigued to know the same philosophy I was attracted to was practiced by a slave and an emperor. How could the same thing appeal to a slave, an emperor, and someone 2,000 years removed from either of them? Who thought of these ideas 2,000 years ago? Why? How could they find answers to problems of living for people who would be alive two millennia later? How did Stoicism come about?

I realized that the only source of the history of Stoicism was written in the first half of the third Century, 600 years after the birth of Stoicism and 150 years after the death of Marcus Aurelius, the last great Stoic. The name of the book is *Lives and Opinions of Eminent Philosophers*, by Diogenes Laertius. While this is the most comprehensive book available on the lives of Stoics (among other philosophers), it is by no means authoritative with many sentences starting with "It is said ..." or "He was said to have ..." or "Some people say ..."

I tried to read other secondary sources hoping to find a more definitive account of events, with little success. It became clear to me that it is not possible to find such a definitive account of events, especially because I am no historian and no scholar of ancient Greek. So I started putting together a plausible history of Stoicism based on more readily available sources.

Even so, it was not easy. There were conflicting accounts. How did Epictetus become lame? His first master broke his legs. No, it was his second master. No, no one broke Epictetus' legs, he had rheumatism. How did Diogenes get to Athens? He was shipwrecked and stranded in Athens. No, he just decided to sell the goods and stay in Athens.

So what I ended up with is an account of Stoic history in the form of stories. In telling the story, I tried to be definitive where I could and tried not to contradict known facts when I couldn't. In describing non-substantive aspects of what happened, I have taken some liberties. It is generally agreed that there was a shipwreck and Diogenes ended up in Athens. Does it matter why the shipwreck happened and whether it happened during the day or the night?

Lack of primary sources forced me to rely on sources like *Lives of Eminent Philosophers* by Diogenes Laertius, Pierre Hadot's excellent books[1], blogs, and writings by modern Stoic scholars such as Massimo Pigliucci, assorted books on Stoicism and, of course, Wikipedia. You can see my source list under "Notes" at the end, although some are secondary sources.

Since the story of Stoicism is not readily accessible to an average reader (except perhaps in academic literature), I thought an anecdotal history based on acceptable sources might interest others as well. After all, it is an improbable story of businessmen, athletes, rich men, poor men, a slave, and an emperor coming together and creating a philosophy of life.

Although initially I wrote the book for my amusement and reference, I thought I would offer it to my fellow Stoics, should they be interested in it as well. I kept the book deliberately short, so it can be read in one sitting if you choose to. So here it is.

Thank you for reading.

Notes

[1] Hadot, Pierre. Inner Citadel; Philosophy as a Way of Life.

(All Cicero's writings can be found in *Delphi Complete Works of Cicero*; Senca's letters in *Letters From a Stoic* (translated by Richard Mott Gummere) and dialogs in *Dialogues* (translated by Aubrey Steward and Damian Stevenson. Kindle editions of these books are available at a low (no) cost from Amazon.com.)

DON'T FORGET!
UNSHAKABLE FREEDOM
A COMPANION VOLUME TO
A FORTUNATE STORM

A Fortunate Storm is the story of how Stoicism came about. UNSHAKABLE FREEDOM shows how Stoic teachings can be used to achieve unshakable freedom in your life right now, no matter what problems you are facing in your life.

Available now at your favorite online bookstore.

READ WHAT OTHERS ARE SAYING ABOUT UNSHAKABLE FREEDOM IN THE FOLLOWING PAGES

Unshakable Freedom: What They are Saying

Choose this book

Chuck Chakrapani reveals for modern eyes what the ancient Stoics knew: True freedom comes from choosing wisely. Here's an aligned piece of advice – choose this book.
Robert Cialdini PhD, Author Influence and *Pre-suasion*

Fast, interesting, and it works

Chuck Chakrapani brings Stoic philosophy to the world of today, the world in which we live, love, compete, win, lose, but never escape. Our world. The early Stoics and those who succeeded them have much to teach, but it takes a thoughtful writer to give us this wisdom in the way WE NEED TO LEARN. Chuck is one of those writers. Read this book …it's fast, interesting, but most of all it WORKS.
Dr. Howard Moskowitz, Chief Science Officer, Mind Genomics Advisors

A timely and readable reminder

We live in a time when happiness and autonomy are commonly equated with higher levels of and options for consumption. This little book is a timely and readable reminder that the path to enjoyment and independence lies elsewhere.
Thomas Dunk PhD, Dean, Faculty of Social Sciences, Brock University

[This book] can change your life for good

Unshakable Freedom is a wonderful guide to those who want real freedom and peace in a complex and challenging world. It also vividly portrays many of the leaders and prominent people who have found success by following these principles. It really can change your life for good.

Ashref Hashim, President, The Blackstone Group

For greater productivity, prosperity and inner peace

In *Unshakable Freedom*, Chuck identifies that the only thing stopping us from being happy is ourselves. The Stoic tenants outlined, if followed, will lead to greater productivity, prosperity, and inner peace for the reader. Thanks to Chuck for the inspiration!

Dr. Kara Mitchelmore,
CEO, Marketing Research & Intelligence Association

Immediately practical

Chuck Chakrapani has written this wonderful book of timeless, immensely practical messages to help us generate powerful real-world impact and remind us how to stay free and appreciative. Unshakable Freedom provides an immediately practical lesson to gain freedom and personal power.

Sabine Steinbrecher, CEO, The Learning Library

Designed to improve quality of life

Unshakable Freedom is about finding peace of mind. Stoic philosophy is a tool to address daily travails - big and small. The author has proposed techniques designed to lead to freedom, happiness, and a better quality of life. I recommend that you go through the book slowly, absorb, and practice.

Naresh Malhotra, CEO Global, Novatrek

ABOUT THE AUTHOR

Dr. Chuck Chakrapani is President of Leger Analytics and Distinguished Visiting Professor at Ryerson University. He has been a long-term, but embarrassingly inconsistent, practitioner of Stoicism. His personal website is ChuckChakrapani.com. For more information on Stoicism, please visit TheStoicGym.com.

Printed in Great Britain
by Amazon